BEST-EVER
VEGETABLE
COOKBOOK

Consultant Editor:
Valerie Ferguson

HERMES
HOUSE

Contents

Introduction

Glorious vegetables – today we can sample and enjoy the widest range from all over the world. Yet seasonal, home-grown produce still cannot be beaten for flavour. So, while taking advantage of the fantastic multi-national displays in cosmopolitan supermarkets, it pays also to buy from local growers who offer freshly harvested produce.

This book suggests tempting ways of cooking both common and less familiar vegetables. It is divided into five sections corresponding to the five main vegetable groups: Onions, Leeks, Shoots & Stems; Beans, Peas & Seeds; Greens; Root Vegetables; and Fruits & Squashes. In some recipes a vegetable may play a starring role, or it may be combined with other ingredients in a harmony of flavours. There are dishes which make fine accompaniments and others which can stand alone as great vegetarian main courses.

As well as being versatile and delicious, vegetables are, of course, vital to good health. We have never been more aware of their importance in our diet, and experts agree that we should eat a high proportion of fresh vegetables each day.

So get cooking, and enjoy your healthy vegetables!

Types of Vegetables

A wonderful variety of fresh vegetables is available in the shops nowadays. The following are used in the recipes in this book.

Onions, Leeks, Shoots & Stems

Onions, obtainable in many different varieties, can be relied upon to bring flavour to almost any savoury dish.

Onions

Leeks are a versatile vegetable with a subtle, oniony flavour. Though available all year round, they are at their best in winter.

Leeks

Asparagus spears, which have an intense, rich flavour, are at their tastiest in early summer.

Asparagus

Mushrooms have a rich flavour. They are versatile and are especially useful in vegetarian recipes.

Chicory is a tight "bud" of usually white, slightly bitter, crisp leaves.

Fennel is a crisp, pale green, aniseed-flavoured, bulb-like vegetable.

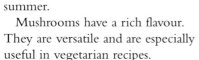

Globe artichokes, best in summer, resemble large thistle heads; the bottom parts of the leaves and the tender heart are edible, but the hairy "choke" is discarded.

Fennel

Beans, Peas & Seeds

Green, runner and broad beans are summer vegetables, although imported green beans are available all year round. They may be steamed or lightly boiled.

Beans & Peas

Okra are small, green pods with a slightly bitter flavour. Peas are nicest when young, sweet and tender, though slightly older peas combine well with other ingredients.

Okra

Sweetcorn is delicious cooked on the cob and eaten with a little butter.

Greens

Broccoli, quick and easy to prepare and cook, is a fine source of vitamins A, C and E.

Broccoli

Brussels sprouts, a popular green winter vegetable, are usually boiled or steamed.

Cabbage, available in many varieties, is a good source of vitamin C. Spring greens are an immature and milder version of this vegetable.

Cabbage

Cauliflower has a pleasant, mild flavour and is prepared and cooked in very little time.

Chard, with its large leaves and thick, succulent stems in green or red, is best steamed.

Spinach is rich in iron. Although tasty on its own, it combines well with other ingredients.

Spinach

Root Vegetables

Beetroot is underestimated as a vegetable: it is especially delicious baked.

Carrots, sweet and fragrant and a good source of vitamin A, are excellent both cooked and raw.

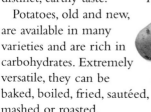

Carrots

Celeriac is a roundish root with a celery flavour.

Jerusalem artichokes, resembling potatoes but much more knobbly, are sweet and nutty-tasting.

Parsnips are sweet-flavoured root vegetables with a distinct, earthy taste.

Parsnips

Potatoes, old and new, are available in many varieties and are rich in carbohydrates. Extremely versatile, they can be baked, boiled, fried, sautéed, mashed or roasted.

Potatoes

Swedes are yellowish in colour and fairly sweet in flavour.

Sweet potatoes are large roots with a sweet taste.

Turnips, ranging from very small to large and mature, have a nutty flavour.

Turnips

Fruits & Squashes

Aubergines differ in colour and shape and have a smoky flavour when cooked.

Aubergines

Courgettes, a type of vegetable marrow, are succulent and tender with a delicate taste.

Peppers, when green, have a fresh flavour; red, yellow and orange peppers are sweeter.

Courgettes

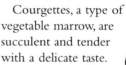

Pumpkins and squashes have fibrous flesh with a gentle, slightly sweet flavour; they are best combined with other ingredients.

Pumpkin

Tomatoes come in a variety of types and sizes. They are excellent alone, raw or cooked, and make a wonderful sauce.

Tomatoes

Techniques

Chopping Onions

Many dishes use chopped onions as an essential flavouring, and for stir-fried dishes it is important to keep the pieces even.

1 Peel the onion. Cut it in half and set it cut side down on a board. Slice through the onion lengthways cutting almost, but not quite, through to the root.

2 Make two horizontal cuts from the stalk end towards the root, but not through it. Cut the onion crossways to form small, even dice.

Skinning & Chopping Tomatoes

It is sometimes recommended that you peel tomatoes before using them.

1 Using a small sharp knife, cut a cross just through the skin at the base of each tomato.

2 Put the tomatoes in a bowl and pour over boiling water. Leave for 20–30 seconds until the skin splits. Drain and transfer to a bowl of cold water. Peel off the skin and chop the flesh into even-size pieces.

COOK'S TIP: Always use firm, fully ripe tomatoes as these will taste better and peel more easily.

Cutting Vegetable Matchsticks

These decorative shapes, also called "julienne", are simple to cut yet look very special.

1 Peel the vegetable and cut across into pieces about 5 cm/2 in long. Shave off the curved edges.

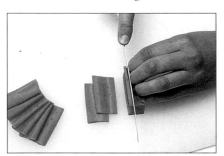

2 Lay each piece flat and cut it lengthways into slices 3 mm/⅛ in thick or less, guiding the side of the knife with your knuckles.

3 Stack the vegetable slices and cut them lengthways into strips about 3 mm/⅛ in thick or less.

Roasting & Peeling Peppers

As peppers have awkward curves, grilling or charring them first makes peeling much easier. This also heightens the sweetness of the flesh.

1 Set the peppers on a rack in a grill pan and grill close to the heat. Turn the peppers to char and blister the skin all over. Alternatively, spear each pepper on a long-handled fork and hold it over a flame, turning it slowly so that the skin is charred and blistered on all sides. Put the peppers in a plastic bag and tie it, or place the peppers under a bowl.

2 Cool – the steam trapped inside the bag or bowl will help loosen the skin. When the peppers are cool enough to handle, peel with the help of a small knife.

Stuffed Parsleyed Onions

An appetizing vegetarian main course or accompaniment to roast meat.

Serves 5

INGREDIENTS
4 large onions
60 ml/4 tbsp cooked rice
20 ml/4 tsp finely chopped fresh parsley,
    plus extra to garnish
60 ml/4 tbsp finely grated strong
    Cheddar cheese
30 ml/2 tbsp olive oil
15 ml/1 tbsp white wine,
    to moisten
salt and freshly ground
    black pepper

1 Preheat the oven to 180°C/350°F/ Gas 4. Cut a slice from the top of each onion and, using a teaspoon, scoop out the centre to leave a fairly thick shell. Place in a single layer in an oiled, shallow ovenproof dish.

2 Combine the rice, parsley, cheese and oil, moistening with enough wine to mix well. Season to taste.

3 Pack the mixture into the onion shells and bake in the oven for 45 minutes or until the onions are just tender. Serve garnished with chopped fresh parsley.

Sweet-&-sour Onions

Serve with roasts and other meat dishes or as part of antipasti.

Serves 4

INGREDIENTS
50 g/2 oz/4 tbsp butter
75 ml/5 tbsp sugar
120 ml/4 fl oz/½ cup white
   wine vinegar
30 ml/2 tbsp balsamic vinegar
675 g/1½ lb small pickling
   onions, peeled
salt and freshly ground
   black pepper

1 Heat the butter in a large saucepan over a gentle heat. Add the sugar and heat until dissolved, stirring constantly.

2 Add the vinegars to the pan with the onions and mix well. Season with salt and pepper.

3 Cover the pan and cook over a moderate heat for 20–25 minutes until the onions are a golden colour and soft when pierced with a knife. Serve hot.

VARIATIONS: This recipe also looks and tastes delicious when made with either yellow or red onions, which are cut either into thin slices or into chunks. Cooking times will vary, depending on the size of the onion pieces.

Leeks in Egg & Lemon Sauce

This sauce has a delicious, fresh taste that brings out the best in the leeks. Be sure to use tender baby leeks for this recipe.

Serves 4

INGREDIENTS
675 g/1½ lb baby leeks
15 ml/1 tbsp cornflour
about 10 ml/2 tsp sugar
2 egg yolks
juice of 1½ lemons
salt and freshly ground black pepper

1 Trim the leeks, slit them from top to bottom and rinse very well under cold water to remove any dirt.

2 Place the leeks in a large saucepan, preferably so that they lie flat on the base. Cover with water and add salt. Bring to the boil, cover and simmer for 4–5 minutes until just tender.

COOK'S TIP: Use some of the green part of the leek for extra colour and flavour.

3 Carefully remove the leeks using a slotted spoon, drain and arrange in a serving dish. Reserve 200 ml/7 fl oz/ scant 1 cup of the cooking liquid.

4 Blend the cornflour with the cooled cooking liquid and place in a small saucepan. Bring to the boil, stirring all the time, and cook over a gentle heat until the sauce thickens slightly. Stir in the sugar and then remove the saucepan from the heat and allow to cool slightly.

5 Beat the egg yolks thoroughly with the lemon juice and stir gradually into the cooled sauce. Cook over a very low heat, stirring all the time, until the sauce is fairly thick. Be careful not to overheat the sauce or it may curdle. As soon as the sauce has thickened, remove the pan from the heat and continue stirring for a minute. Taste and add salt or sugar as necessary. Cool slightly.

6 Stir the cooled sauce with a wooden spoon. Pour the sauce over the leeks. Cover and chill well for at least 2 hours before serving garnished with a few twists of freshly ground black pepper.

Roasted Fennel with Pernod & Walnut Salad

The aniseed flavour of fennel is enhanced with Pernod, which makes an unusual warm salad dressing.

Serves 4

INGREDIENTS
1.5 ml/¼ tsp butter
4 fennel bulbs, trimmed
60 ml/4 tbsp Pernod
30 ml/2 tbsp olive oil
10 ml/2 tsp soft light brown sugar
salt and freshly ground
    black pepper

FOR THE SALAD
30 ml/2 tbsp olive oil
50 g/2 oz/½ cup walnut
    halves, broken
2.5 ml/½ tsp mustard seeds
15 ml/1 tbsp Pernod
3 handfuls salad leaves
1 bunch radishes, with small
    leaves left on

1 Preheat the oven to 190°C/375°F/ Gas 5. Use the butter to grease a large, shallow casserole. Cook the fennel bulbs in a saucepan of lightly salted boiling water until tender, and drain.

VARIATION: This recipe is also very good made with celery or chicory instead of fennel.

2 Cut each fennel bulb lengthways into quarters. Arrange them in a single layer in the casserole. Pour the Pernod and oil over, sprinkle with the sugar and season with salt and pepper. Cover and bake for about 30 minutes, basting from time to time.

3 To make the salad, warm the olive oil in a small pan. Remove from the heat and stir in the walnut pieces and mustard seeds. Return the pan to the heat, cover and heat until the mustard seeds start to pop. Mix in the Pernod.

4 Arrange the salad leaves on a platter. Slice some of the radishes and scatter them, with the whole radishes, over the lettuce. Top with the roasted fennel. Pour over the warm dressing and serve at once.

COOK'S TIP: When buying fennel, choose pale green to white, well-rounded roots for the best flavour.

Baked Chicory with Parma Ham

Although chicory is too harshly flavoured for some tastes, simmering it before baking eliminates any bitterness, giving it a mild flavour.

Serves 4

INGREDIENTS

4 heads chicory
25 g/1 oz/2 tbsp butter
250 ml/8 fl oz/1 cup vegetable or
    chicken stock
4 slices Parma ham
75 g/3 oz/6 tbsp mascarpone cheese
50 g/2 oz Emmenthal or Cheddar
    cheese, sliced
salt and freshly ground
    black pepper

1 Preheat the oven to 180°C/350°F/ Gas 4. Grease an ovenproof dish. Trim the heads of chicory and remove the central cores.

2 Melt the butter in a large saucepan and gently sauté the chicory over a moderate heat for 4–5 minutes, turning occasionally, until the outer leaves begin to turn transparent.

3 Add the stock and a little seasoning, bring to the boil and then cover and simmer gently for 5–6 minutes until the chicory is almost tender.

4 Remove the chicory using a slotted spoon. Lay out the Parma ham slices and place one piece of chicory on each of the slices. Roll up and place, side by side, in a single layer in the prepared dish.

5 Simmer the stock until it is reduced by about half and then remove from the heat. Stir in the mascarpone and pour the sauce over the chicory. Lay the slices of Emmenthal or Cheddar over the top and bake for about 15 minutes until the top is golden and the sauce is bubbling. Serve hot.

Stuffed Artichokes

An Italian-style dish that makes a superb starter for a dinner party.

Serves 6

INGREDIENTS
1 lemon
6 large globe artichokes
1 garlic clove, cut into 3 or 4 pieces
sprigs of fresh flat leaf parsley
45 ml/3 tbsp olive oil

FOR THE STUFFING
2 slices white bread, crusts removed
   (about 50 g/2 oz)
3 canned anchovy fillets, finely chopped
2 garlic cloves, finely chopped
30 ml/2 tbsp capers, rinsed and
   finely chopped
45 ml/3 tbsp finely chopped fresh
   flat leaf parsley
60 ml/4 tbsp plain breadcrumbs
60 ml/4 tbsp olive oil
salt and freshly ground black pepper

1 To prepare the stuffing, soak the white bread in a little water for 5 minutes. Squeeze dry. Place in a bowl with the other stuffing ingredients and mix. Preheat the oven to 190°C/375°F/Gas 5.

2 Squeeze the lemon, and put the juice and the squeezed halves in a large bowl of cold water. Wash the artichokes and prepare them one at a time. Cut off only the tip from the stem. Peel the stem with a small knife, pulling upwards towards the leaves.

3 Pull off the small leaves around the stem, and continue snapping off the upper part of the dark outer leaves until you reach the taller inner leaves. Cut off the topmost part of these leaves with a sharp knife.

4 Open the artichoke slightly by spreading the leaves apart to get at the inner bristly "choke". Cut around it with the knife, and scrape it out with a small spoon. This forms a cavity inside the artichoke leaves. As soon as each artichoke has been prepared, place it in the bowl of acidulated water. This will prevent it from darkening.

5 Place the garlic and a parsley sprig in a baking dish large enough to hold the artichokes upright in one layer. Pour in cold water to a depth of 1 cm/½ in. Remove the artichokes from the bowl, drain quickly, and fill the cavities with the stuffing.

6 Place the stuffed artichokes upside down in the dish and pour a little oil over each one. Cover the dish tightly with foil and bake for about 1 hour or until the artichokes are tender. Serve immediately, garnished with fresh parsley sprigs.

Asparagus Rolls with Herb Butter Sauce

For a taste sensation, try tender asparagus spears wrapped in crisp filo pastry. The buttery herb sauce makes the perfect accompaniment.

Serves 2

INGREDIENTS
4 sheets filo pastry,
    thawed if frozen
50 g/2 oz/4 tbsp butter, melted
16 young asparagus spears, trimmed
salad, to serve

FOR THE SAUCE
2 shallots, finely chopped
1 bay leaf
150 ml/¼ pint/⅔ cup dry white wine
175 g/6 oz/¾ cup butter, softened
15 ml/1 tbsp chopped fresh herbs
salt and freshly ground
    black pepper
snipped chives, to garnish

1 Preheat the oven to 200°C/400°F/ Gas 6. Brush each filo sheet with some of the melted butter. Fold one corner of the sheet down to the bottom edge to give a wedge shape.

2 Lay four asparagus spears on top at the longest edge and roll up towards the shortest edge. Using the remaining filo and asparagus spears, make three more rolls in the same way.

3 Lay the rolls on a greased baking sheet. Brush with the remaining melted butter. Bake in the oven for 8 minutes or until golden.

4 To make the sauce, put the chopped shallots, bay leaf and wine into a pan. Cover and cook over a high heat until the wine is reduced to about 45–60 ml/3–4 tbsp.

5 Strain the wine and shallot mixture into a bowl. Whisk in the butter, a little at a time, until the sauce is smooth and glossy.

6 Stir in the herbs and add salt and pepper to taste. Return the sauce to the pan and keep warm. Serve the rolls on individual plates with salad. Serve the butter sauce separately, sprinkled with a few snipped chives.

l Coconut Mushrooms

A simple and delicious mushroom dish which may be served with almost any Asian meal as well as with plainly grilled or roasted meats and poultry.

Serves 3–4

INGREDIENTS
30 ml/2 tbsp groundnut oil
2 garlic cloves,
    finely chopped
2 fresh red chillies, seeded and sliced
    into rings
3 shallots, finely chopped
225 g/8 oz/3¼ cups brown-cap
    mushrooms, thickly sliced
150 ml/¼ pint/⅔ cup
    coconut milk
30 ml/2 tbsp chopped
    fresh coriander
salt and freshly ground
    black pepper

1 Heat a wok until hot, add the oil and swirl it around. Add the garlic and chillies, then stir-fry for a few seconds.

2 Add the shallots to the wok and stir-fry for 2–3 minutes until softened. Add the mushrooms and stir-fry for 3 minutes.

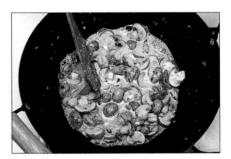

3 Pour in the coconut milk and bring to the boil. Boil rapidly over a high heat until the liquid is reduced by half and coats the mushrooms. Taste and adjust the seasoning if necessary.

VARIATION: Use snipped fresh chives instead of coriander for this dish, if you wish.

4 Sprinkle over the chopped fresh coriander and toss the spiced coconut mushrooms gently to mix. Transfer to a warmed dish and serve immediately.

COOK'S TIP: For a hotter curry leave in some of the chilli seeds.

Oriental Green Beans

A perfect way to enliven green beans, this is good served hot or cold.

Serves 4

INGREDIENTS
450 g/1 lb/3 cups green beans
15 ml/1 tbsp olive oil
5 ml/1 tsp sesame oil
2 garlic cloves, crushed
2.5 cm/1 in piece fresh root ginger,
    peeled and finely chopped
30 ml/2 tbsp dark soy sauce

1 Steam the beans over a saucepan of boiling salted water for 6 minutes or until just tender.

2 Meanwhile, heat the olive and sesame oils in a heavy-based saucepan, add the garlic and sauté for 2 minutes.

3 Stir in the ginger and soy sauce and cook, stirring constantly, for a further 2–3 minutes until the liquid has reduced. Transfer the warm beans to a serving dish, then pour the ginger and soy sauce mixture over them.

4 Leave the beans to stand for a few minutes to allow all the flavours to mingle before serving.

VARIATION: Substitute other green beans, if you wish. Runner beans and other flat varieties should be cut diagonally into thick slices before steaming.

Runner Beans with Garlic

Flageolet beans and garlic add a French flavour to this simple side dish.

Serves 4

INGREDIENTS
225 g/8 oz/1¼ cups flageolet beans,
    soaked in water overnight, then drained
15 ml/1 tbsp olive oil
25 g/1 oz/2 tbsp butter
1 onion, finely chopped
1–2 garlic cloves, crushed
3–4 tomatoes, peeled and chopped
350 g/12 oz/2¼ cups runner beans
150 ml/¼ pint/⅔ cup white wine
150 ml/¼ pint/⅔ cup vegetable stock
30 ml/2 tbsp chopped fresh parsley
salt and freshly ground black pepper

1 Place the flageolet beans in a large saucepan of fresh water, bring to the boil and simmer for 45 minutes–1 hour until tender. Drain.

2 Heat the oil and butter in a large frying pan and sauté the onion and garlic for 3–4 minutes until soft but not browned. Add the chopped tomatoes and continue cooking over a gentle heat until they are soft.

3 Slice the runner beans. Stir the flageolet beans into the onion and tomato mixture, then add the runner beans, white wine, stock and a little salt. Stir well. Cover and simmer for 5–10 minutes until the runner beans are tender but not too soft.

4 Increase the heat to reduce the liquid, then stir in the parsley and season with a little more salt, if necessary, and freshly ground pepper before serving.

Peas with Lettuce & Onion

An especially good recipe for not-so-young peas.

Serves 4–6

INGREDIENTS
15 g/½ oz/1 tbsp butter
1 small onion, finely chopped
1 small round lettuce
450 g/1 lb/4 cups shelled fresh peas
   (from about 1.5 kg/3½ lb peas) or thawed
   frozen peas
salt and freshly ground black pepper

1 Melt the butter in a heavy saucepan. Add the onion and cook over a medium-low heat for about 3 minutes until just softened.

2 Cut the lettuce in half through the core, then place cut side down on a board and slice into thin strips. Place the lettuce strips on top of the onion in the pan and add the peas and 45 ml/3 tbsp water. Season lightly with salt and pepper.

3 Cover the pan tightly and cook the lettuce and peas over a low heat until the peas are tender – fresh peas will take 10–20 minutes, frozen peas about 10 minutes.

Broad Beans with Cream & Chives

Even people who claim to dislike broad beans will enjoy this dish.

Serves 4–6

INGREDIENTS
450 g/1 lb/3¼ cups shelled broad beans
   (from about 2 kg/4½ lb broad beans)
90 ml/6 tbsp whipping cream or
   crème fraîche
salt and freshly ground black pepper
finely snipped chives, to garnish

1 Bring a large pan of salted water to the boil over a medium-high heat and add the beans.

2 Bring back to the boil, then reduce the heat slightly and boil the beans gently for about 8 minutes until just tender. Drain and refresh in cold water, then drain again.

3 To remove the skins, make an opening along one side of each bean with the tip of a knife and gently squeeze out the green bean.

4 Put the beans in a saucepan with the cream or crème fraîche and seasoning, cover and heat gently. Sprinkle with the chives and serve.

Right: Peas with Lettuce & Onion (top); Broad Beans with Cream & Chives

Okra with Tomato & Coriander

A spicy vegetarian dish that is delicious served either with other vegetable dishes or as an accompaniment to meat.

Serves 4

INGREDIENTS
350 g/12 oz okra
5–6 tomatoes
2 small onions
2 garlic cloves, crushed
1 green chilli, seeded
5 ml/1 tsp paprika
small handful of fresh coriander,
    plus extra to garnish
30 ml/2 tbsp sunflower oil
juice of 1 lemon
salt and freshly ground black pepper

1 Trim the okra and then cut into 1 cm/½ in lengths. Peel and seed the tomatoes and chop roughly.

2 Roughly chop one of the onions and place in a food processor or blender with the garlic, chilli, paprika, coriander and 60 ml/4 tbsp water. Blend to a paste.

3 Thinly slice the second onion and fry in the oil for 5–6 minutes until golden brown. Transfer to a plate with a slotted spoon. Reduce the heat and pour in the onion and coriander mixture. Cook for 1–2 minutes, stirring frequently.

4 Add the okra, tomatoes, lemon juice, seasoning and about 120 ml/ 4 fl oz/½ cup water. Stir well to mix, cover tightly and simmer over a low heat for about 15 minutes until the okra is tender. Transfer to a serving dish, sprinkle with the onion rings and coriander, and serve.

etcorn Fritters

There is no doubt that freshly cooked sweetcorn is best for this recipe.
Do not add salt to the water, because this toughens the skin.

Makes 20

INGREDIENTS
2 fresh corn cobs or 350 g/12 oz can
   sweetcorn kernels
2 macadamia nuts or
   4 almonds
1 garlic clove
1 onion, chopped
1 cm/½ in piece fresh galangal,
   peeled and sliced
5 ml/1 tsp ground coriander
30–45 ml/2–3 tbsp groundnut oil
3 eggs, beaten
30 ml/2 tbsp desiccated coconut
2 spring onions, finely shredded
a few celery leaves, finely shredded,
   plus extra whole leaves to
   garnish (optional)
salt

1 Cook the corn cobs in boiling
water for 7–8 minutes. Drain, cool
slightly and, using a sharp knife, strip
the kernels from the cobs. If using
canned sweetcorn, drain well.

2 Grind the macadamia nuts or
almonds, garlic, onion, galangal and
coriander to a fine paste in a food
processor or pestle and mortar. Heat a
little of the oil in a small, heavy-based
pan, and fry the paste until it gives off
a spicy aroma.

3 Put the beaten eggs in a large bowl,
and add the fried spices with the
coconut, spring onions and celery
leaves, if using. Add the corn kernels
and salt to taste.

4 Heat the remaining oil in a shallow
frying pan. Drop large spoonfuls of
batter into the pan and cook for 2–3
minutes until golden. Flip the fritters
over with a fish slice and cook until
golden brown and crispy.

COOK'S TIP: Galangal, a root used
in Far Eastern cooking, is a member
of the ginger family. Use fresh root
ginger if you are unable to find it.

5 Cook only three or four fritters at a time and drain them on crumpled kitchen paper. Keep them warm in a medium hot oven until you are ready to serve. Garnish with celery leaves, if liked.

VARIATION: These fritters could also be made using grated carrot, courgette and red pepper instead of the sweetcorn. Finely chop the pepper if you are unable to grate it.

Spinach & Cannellini Beans

A fine, hearty dish to serve on a cold evening, this also works well with other dried beans such as haricots or chick-peas.

Serves 4

INGREDIENTS
225 g/8 oz/1¼ cups cannellini beans,
   soaked in water overnight
60 ml/4 tbsp olive oil
1 slice white bread
1 onion, chopped
3–4 tomatoes, peeled and chopped
a good pinch of paprika
450 g/1 lb spinach
1 garlic clove, halved
salt and freshly ground
   black pepper
chunks of crusty bread,
   to serve

1 Drain the beans, place in a saucepan and cover with water. Bring to the boil and boil rapidly for 10 minutes. Cover and simmer for about 1 hour until the beans are tender. Drain.

2 Heat 30 ml/2 tbsp of the oil in a frying pan and fry the bread until golden brown. Transfer to a plate.

3 Fry the onion in 15 ml/1 tbsp of the oil over a gentle heat until soft but not brown, then add the tomatoes and continue cooking over a gentle heat.

4 Heat the remaining oil in a large pan, stir in the paprika and then add the spinach. Cover and cook for a few minutes until the spinach has wilted.

5 Add the onion and tomato mixture to the spinach, mix well and stir in the cannellini beans. Season to taste with salt and freshly ground black pepper.

6 Place the garlic and fried bread in a food processor and process until smooth. Stir into the spinach and bean mixture. Add 150 ml/¼ pint/⅔ cup cold water, cover and simmer gently for 20–30 minutes, adding more water if necessary. Serve hot with chunks of crusty bread.

Spinach & Roast Garlic Salad

Don't worry about the amount of garlic in this salad. During roasting the garlic becomes sweet and subtle and loses its pungent taste.

Serves 4

INGREDIENTS
12 garlic cloves, unpeeled
60 ml/4 tbsp extra virgin olive oil
450 g/1 lb baby spinach leaves
50 g/2 oz/½ cup pine nuts, lightly toasted
juice of ½ lemon
salt and freshly ground black pepper

1 Preheat the oven to 190°C/375°F/ Gas 5. Place the garlic in a small roasting tin, toss in 30 ml/2 tbsp of the olive oil and bake for about 15 minutes until the garlic cloves are slightly charred around the edges.

2 While it is still warm, tip the garlic into a salad bowl. Add the spinach, pine nuts, lemon juice, remaining olive oil and a little salt.

3 Toss well and add black pepper to taste. Serve immediately, inviting guests to squeeze the softened garlic purée out of the skin to eat.

COOK'S TIP: If spinach is to be served raw in a salad, the leaves need to be young and tender. Wash them well, drain and pat dry with kitchen paper.

Braised Spring Greens

This dish can be served as a vegetable accompaniment or it can be enjoyed simply on its own with some warm, crusty bread.

Serves 4

INGREDIENTS
30 ml/2 tbsp olive oil
25 g/1 oz/2 tbsp butter
75 g/3 oz/½ cup rindless smoked streaky
    bacon, chopped
1 large onion, thinly sliced
2 garlic cloves, finely chopped
250 ml/8 fl oz/1 cup dry
    white wine
900 g/2 lb spring greens, shredded
salt and freshly ground black pepper

1 In a large frying pan, heat the oil and butter and add the bacon. Fry for 2 minutes, then add the onion and garlic and fry for a further 3 minutes until the onion is beginning to soften.

2 Add the dry white wine and simmer vigorously for 2 minutes until reduced to about two-thirds of its original volume.

3 Lower the heat and add the spring greens and salt and pepper. Cook over a gentle heat for about 15 minutes until the greens are tender. (Cover the pan so that the greens retain their colour.) Serve hot.

VARIATION: This dish would work just as well using shredded red cabbage and red wine. Leave to simmer for 10 minutes longer, as red cabbage leaves are slightly tougher than the spring greens.

Stuffed Cabbage Parcels

These attractive, tied parcels, served with a tomato and onion sauce, make a tasty and colourful meal.

Serves 4

INGREDIENTS
12 large outer green
   cabbage leaves
4 spring onions
30 ml/2 tbsp vegetable oil
1 small onion, finely chopped
2 garlic cloves, crushed
400 g/14 oz can plum tomatoes
pinch of sugar
salt and freshly ground
   black pepper

FOR THE STUFFING
4 dried Chinese mushrooms, soaked
   in hot water until soft
50 g/2 oz cellophane noodles,
   soaked in hot water until soft
450 g/1 lb minced pork
4 spring onions, finely chopped
2 garlic cloves, finely chopped
30 ml/2 tbsp fish sauce

1 To make the stuffing, drain the mushrooms, and remove and discard the stems. Coarsely chop the caps and put them in a bowl.

2 Drain the noodles and cut them into short lengths. Add the noodles to the bowl with the pork, chopped spring onions and garlic. Season with the fish sauce and add pepper to taste. Set aside.

3 Cut off the tough stem from each cabbage leaf. Blanch the leaves, a few at a time, in a saucepan of boiling salted water for about 1 minute. Remove the leaves from the pan and refresh under cold water. Drain and dry on kitchen paper. Add the spring onions to the boiling water and blanch in the same fashion. Drain well.

4 Fill one of the cabbage leaves with a generous spoonful of the pork and noodle filling. Roll up the leaf sufficiently to enclose the filling, then tuck in the sides and continue rolling the leaf to make a tight parcel. Make 11 more parcels in the same way.

5 Split each whole, blanched spring onion lengthways into three strands by cutting through the bulb and then tearing upwards. Tie each of the cabbage parcels with a length of spring onion.

6 Heat the oil in a pan. Add the onion and garlic and fry for 5 minutes. Tip the tomatoes and their juice into a bowl, mash, then stir into the onion mixture. Cook for 20 minutes. Season with salt, pepper and sugar, then bring to simmering point.

7 Cook the cabbage parcels in a bamboo steamer or wok fitted with a steamer rack for 20–25 minutes or until the filling is cooked, adding more water if necessary. To serve, place some sauce on a plate and top with the parcels.

Provençal Chard Omelette

This traditional, flat omelette can also be made with fresh spinach, but chard leaves are typically used in Provence. It is delicious served with small, black Niçoise olives and a tomato and basil salad.

Serves 6

INGREDIENTS
675 g/1½ lb chard leaves without stalks
60 ml/4 tbsp olive oil
1 large onion, sliced
5 eggs
salt and freshly ground black pepper
sprig of fresh parsley, to garnish

1 Wash the chard well in several changes of water and pat dry. Stack four or five leaves at a time and slice across into thin ribbons. Steam the chard until wilted, then drain in a sieve and press out any liquid with the back of a spoon.

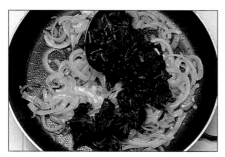

2 ·Heat 30 ml/2 tbsp of the oil in a large frying pan. Add the onion and cook over a medium-low heat for about 10 minutes until soft, stirring occasionally. Add the chard and cook for a further 2–4 minutes until the leaves are tender.

3 In a large bowl, beat the eggs and season with salt and pepper, then stir in the cooked vegetables.

4 Heat the remaining oil in a large, non-stick frying pan over a medium-high heat. Pour in the egg mixture and reduce the heat to medium-low. Cook the omelette, covered, for 5–7 minutes until the egg mixture is set around the edges and almost set on top.

VARIATION: This omelette can also be made using 50 g/2 oz each of cooked, diced ham, cooked peas and cooked, chopped carrots added at step 3. Top the omelette with grated cheese, if you like.

5 To turn the omelette over, loosen the edges and slide it on to a large plate. Place the frying pan over the omelette and, holding them tightly, carefully invert the pan and plate together. Lift off the plate and continue cooking for a further 2–3 minutes. Slide the omelette on to a serving plate, garnish with parsley, and serve, cut into wedges.

Brussels Sprouts Stir-fry

Cooked in this way, Brussels sprouts are really full-flavoured and crisp.

Serves 6

INGREDIENTS
450 g/1 lb small Brussels sprouts
3 spring onions
2 garlic cloves
1 small yellow pepper
30 ml/2 tbsp groundnut or
    sunflower oil
30 ml/2 tbsp light soy sauce
15 ml/1 tbsp sesame oil
good pinch of
    granulated sugar
30 ml/2 tbsp sesame
    seeds, toasted
freshly ground black pepper

1 Trim the sprouts. Slice the spring onions. Crush the garlic. Seed and slice the yellow pepper.

2 Heat the oil in a wok until quite hot, add the sprouts and stir-fry quickly for 2 minutes.

3 Add the spring onions, garlic and yellow pepper and fry for another 2 minutes, stirring constantly.

4 Toss in the soy sauce, sesame oil and sugar. Season to taste with pepper. Scatter over the sesame seeds and serve the Brussels sprouts immediately.

Broccoli & Cauliflower in Cider Sauce

A delicious and unusual sauce flavoured with tamari and apple mint.

Serves 4

INGREDIENTS
1 large onion, chopped
2 large carrots, chopped
1 large garlic clove
15 ml/1 tbsp dill seeds
4 large sprigs of fresh apple mint
30 ml/2 tbsp olive oil
30 ml/2 tbsp plain flour
300 ml/½ pint/1¼ cups dry cider
500 g/1¼ lb broccoli florets
500 g/1¼ lb cauliflower florets
30 ml/2 tbsp tamari
   (Japanese soy sauce)
10 ml/2 tsp mint jelly

1 Sauté the onion, carrots, garlic, dill seeds and apple-mint leaves in the olive oil until the vegetables are nearly cooked. Stir in the flour and cook for about 30 seconds. Pour in the cider and simmer until the sauce looks glossy.

2 Cook the broccoli and cauliflower in separate pans of boiling salted water until just tender. Drain thoroughly.

3 Pour the sauce into a food processor and add the tamari and mint jelly. Blend until coarsely puréed. Pour over the broccoli and cauliflower, and serve hot.

Potato Pan Gratin

Sliced potatoes layered with mustard butter and thyme are baked until golden. This is a perfect accompaniment to a vegetarian or meat roast.

Serves 4

INGREDIENTS

4 large potatoes, about 900 g/2 lb
   total weight
25 g/1 oz/2 tbsp butter
15 ml/1 tbsp olive oil
2 large garlic cloves, crushed
30 ml/2 tbsp Dijon mustard
15 ml/1 tbsp lemon juice
30 ml/2 tbsp fresh
   thyme leaves
50 ml/2 fl oz/¼ cup vegetable stock
salt and freshly ground
   black pepper

1 Peel and thinly slice the potatoes using a sharp knife or a slicing attachment on a food processor. Place in a bowl of cold water to prevent them discolouring.

VARIATION: Any root vegetables can be used in this dish: try celeriac, parsnips, swede or turnips.

2 Preheat the oven to 200°C/400°F/ Gas 6. Heat the butter and oil in a deep, ovenproof frying pan or skillet. Add the garlic and cook gently for 3 minutes until light golden, stirring constantly. Stir in the mustard, lemon juice and 15 ml/1 tbsp of the thyme. Remove from the heat and pour the mixture into a jug.

3 Drain the potatoes and pat dry with kitchen paper. Place a layer of potatoes in the frying pan or skillet, season and pour over one-third of the butter mixture. Cover with another layer of potatoes, season and pour over another third of the butter mixture.

4 Arrange a final layer of potatoes on top, pour over the rest of the butter mixture and then the stock. Season once more and sprinkle with the remaining thyme.

5 Cover the layered potatoes with greaseproof paper and bake for 1 hour. Remove the paper and cook for a further 15 minutes or until golden brown and just beginning to crisp at the edges. Serve hot.

...zed Sweet Potatoes

Fried sweet potatoes with a scrumptious candied coating.

Serves 4

INGREDIENTS
900 g/2 lb sweet potatoes
50 g/2 oz/4 tbsp butter
45 ml/3 tbsp oil
2 garlic cloves, crushed
2 pieces stem ginger, finely chopped
10 ml/2 tsp ground allspice
15 ml/1 tbsp syrup from the ginger jar
10 ml/2 tsp chopped fresh thyme, plus a few
    sprigs to garnish
salt and cayenne pepper

1 Peel the sweet potatoes and cut into 1 cm/½ in cubes. Melt the butter with the oil in a large frying pan. Add the sweet potato cubes and fry, stirring frequently, for about 10 minutes until they are just soft.

2 Stir in the garlic, ginger and allspice. Cook over a gentle heat, stirring, for 5 minutes more.

3 Stir in the ginger syrup, salt, a generous pinch of cayenne pepper and the chopped thyme. Stir for 1–2 minutes more, then serve scattered with thyme sprigs.

Right: Glazed Sweet Potatoes (top); Roasted Root Vegetables

Roasted Root Vegetables

These easily prepared vegetables can be cooked alongside a joint.

Serves 4

INGREDIENTS
3 parsnips, cut into chunky sticks
3 potatoes, cut into chunks
3 carrots, cut into chunks
3 sweet potatoes, cut into chunks
60 ml/4 tbsp olive oil
8 shallots
2 garlic cloves, sliced
10 ml/2 tsp white mustard seeds
10 ml/2 tsp coriander seeds, lightly crushed
5 ml/1 tsp cumin seeds
2 bay leaves
salt and freshly ground black pepper

1 Preheat the oven to 190°C/375°F/ Gas 5. Cook the root vegetables in boiling salted water for 2 minutes, then drain thoroughly.

2 Pour the oil into a large, heavy roasting tin and place over a moderate heat. Add the vegetables, shallots and garlic and fry, tossing them until they are pale golden at the edges.

3 Add the mustard, coriander and cumin seeds with the bay leaves. Cook for 1 minute, then season. Transfer to the oven and roast for 45 minutes, turning occasionally, until the vegetables are crisp and golden. Serve.

Parsnip & Carrot Fricassée

An excellent main course accompaniment to meat or fish.

Serves 4–6

INGREDIENTS
4 parsnips, cut into chunky sticks
4 carrots, cut into chunky sticks
1 onion, sliced
30 ml/2 tbsp pine nuts or flaked almonds,
   lightly toasted
salt and freshly ground
   black pepper
sprigs of fresh tarragon,
   to garnish

FOR THE SAUCE
40 g/1½ oz/3 tbsp butter
40 g/1½ oz/⅓ cup plain flour
300 ml/½ pint/1¼ cups milk
130 g/4½ oz goat's cheese
15 ml/1 tbsp chopped fresh or
   2.5 ml/½ tsp dried tarragon

1 Put the parsnips, carrots and onion into a saucepan. Season, cover with cold water and bring to the boil. Lower the heat and simmer for 10 minutes. Drain, reserving 200 ml/ 7 fl oz/scant 1 cup of the cooking water. Put the vegetables in a hot dish.

2 Melt the butter in a clean pan and stir in the flour. Cook for 1 minute, stirring, then whisk in the reserved vegetable water and the milk. Heat, whisking, until the sauce boils and thickens. Simmer gently for 2 minutes.

3 Remove from the heat and stir in the goat's cheese, tarragon and seasoning. Pour the sauce over the vegetables, sprinkle with the nuts, and serve garnished with tarragon.

Purée of Root Vegetables

This sophisticated, subtly coloured combination of root vegetables is delicious with both meat and fish.

Serves 4

INGREDIENTS
225 g/8 oz celeriac, peeled
115 g/4 oz swede, peeled
225 g/8 oz turnips, peeled or scraped
225 g/8 oz carrots, peeled or scraped
1 small shallot
25 g/1 oz/2 tbsp butter
15 ml/1 tbsp single cream
1.5 ml/¼ tsp freshly
   grated nutmeg
salt and freshly ground
   black pepper
fresh chives, to garnish

1 Cut all four root vegetables into bite-size pieces. Finely chop the shallot.

2 Place all the root vegetables and the shallot in a pan of very lightly salted, boiling water. Cook for 8 minutes until tender but still firm.

3 Drain in a colander and place in a blender or food processor with the butter and cream. Process to a fine purée, then season with salt, pepper and nutmeg. Spoon directly into four serving bowls. Garnish with fresh chives and serve immediately.

Artichoke Rösti

Grated Jerusalem artichokes are mixed with potatoes to create a crisp
fried "cake". Serve with grilled bacon or fried eggs.

Serves 4–6

INGREDIENTS
450 g/1 lb Jerusalem artichokes
juice of 1 lemon
450 g/1 lb potatoes
about 50 g/2 oz/4 tbsp butter
salt and freshly ground black pepper

1 Peel the artichokes and place in a
saucepan of water with the lemon
juice and a pinch of salt. Bring to the
boil and cook for about 5 minutes
until barely tender.

2 Peel the potatoes and boil in a
separate pan of salted water until
barely tender – they will take slightly
longer than the artichokes.

3 Drain and cool both vegetables,
then grate them into a bowl. Mix
them with your fingers, without
breaking them up too much.

4 Melt the butter in a frying pan. Add
the artichoke mixture, spreading it out.
Cook gently for about 10 minutes.
Invert the "cake" on to a plate and
slide back into the pan. Cook for
about 10 minutes until golden. Add
pepper, and serve.

Beetroot & Celeriac Gratin

This combination of root vegetables makes a stunning side dish.

Serves 6

INGREDIENTS
350 g/12 oz raw beetroot
350 g/12 oz celeriac
4 fresh thyme sprigs, plus extra,
    to garnish
6 juniper berries, crushed
120 ml/4 fl oz/½ cup fresh
    orange juice
120 ml/4 fl oz/½ cup
    vegetable stock
salt and freshly ground black pepper

1 Preheat the oven to 190°C/375°F/
Gas 5. Peel and slice the beetroot very
finely. Quarter and peel the celeriac
and slice very finely.

2 Fill a 25 cm/10 in diameter, cast-
iron, ovenproof frying pan or skillet
with alternate layers of beetroot and
celeriac slices, sprinkling with thyme,
juniper and seasoning between
each layer.

3 Mix the orange juice and stock
together and pour over the gratin.
Place over a medium heat and bring
to the boil. Boil for 2 minutes.

4 Cover with foil and place in the
oven for 15–20 minutes. Remove the
foil and raise the oven temperature to
200°C/400°F/Gas 6. Cook for a
further 10 minutes. Serve garnished
with the reserved thyme.

Tomato & Basil Tart

This tart is similar to a pizza, but uses shortcrust pastry instead of yeast dough for the base.

Serves 6–8

INGREDIENTS
175 g/6 oz/1½ cups flour
2.5 ml/½ tsp salt
115 g/4 oz/½ cup butter or margarine, chilled
30 ml/2 tbsp extra virgin olive oil

FOR THE FILLING
175 g/6 oz Mozzarella cheese, sliced as
    thinly as possible
12 fresh basil leaves
4–5 medium tomatoes, cut into 5 mm/
    ¼ in slices
60 ml/4 tbsp freshly grated Parmesan cheese
salt and freshly ground black pepper

1 Make the pastry by sifting the flour and salt into a mixing bowl. Using a pastry blender, cut the butter or margarine into the dry ingredients until the mixture resembles coarse breadcrumbs. Add 45 ml/3 tbsp cold water, and combine with a fork until the dough holds together. If it is too crumbly, mix in a little more water.

2 Gather the dough into a ball and flatten it into a disc. Wrap in greaseproof paper and refrigerate for at least 40 minutes. Preheat the oven to 190°C/375°F/Gas 5.

3 Roll out the pastry between two sheets of greaseproof paper to a thickness of 5 mm/¼ in. Use it to line a 28 cm/11 in tart tin, trimming the edges evenly. Refrigerate for 20 minutes. Prick the bottom all over with a fork.

4 Line the pastry case with a sheet of baking parchment. Fill with dried beans. Place the tin on a baking sheet and bake for 15 minutes. Remove from the oven. Leave the oven on.

5 Remove the beans and paper. Brush the pastry with some oil. Line with the Mozzarella. Tear half of the basil into pieces and sprinkle on top.

6 Arrange the tomato slices over the cheese. Dot with the remaining whole basil leaves. Sprinkle with salt and pepper, Parmesan and oil. Bake for about 35 minutes. If the cheese exudes a lot of liquid during baking, tilt the pan and spoon it off to keep the pastry from becoming soggy. Serve hot or at room temperature.

Roasted Plum Tomatoes

These are so simple to prepare yet taste absolutely wonderful.

Serves 4

INGREDIENTS
8 plum tomatoes, halved
12 garlic cloves
60 ml/4 tbsp extra virgin olive oil
3 bay leaves
salt and freshly ground
    black pepper
45 ml/3 tbsp fresh oregano leaves,
    to garnish

1 Preheat the oven to 230°C/450°F/
Gas 8. Select an ovenproof dish that
will hold all the tomatoes snugly in a
single layer. Place the tomatoes in the
dish and push the whole, unpeeled
garlic cloves between them.

2 Brush the tomatoes with the oil,
add the bay leaves and sprinkle black
pepper over the top. Bake for about
45 minutes until the tomatoes have
softened and are sizzling in the pan;
they should be slightly charred around
the edges.

3 Season with salt and a little more
black pepper, if needed. Garnish with
oregano and serve.

COOK'S TIP: Use ripe plum
tomatoes with their stalks on for
this recipe, as they keep their shape
and do not fall apart when roasted
at such a high temperature.

Stuffed Peppers

The couscous stuffing gives this dish a Middle Eastern flavour.

Serves 6

INGREDIENTS
6 peppers
25 g/1 oz/2 tbsp butter
1 onion, finely chopped
5 ml/1 tsp olive oil
2.5 ml/½ tsp salt
175 g/6 oz/1 cup couscous
25 g/1 oz/2 tbsp raisins
30 ml/2 tbsp chopped fresh mint
1 egg yolk
salt and freshly ground black pepper
fresh mint leaves, to garnish

1 Preheat the oven to 200°C/400°F/
Gas 6. Slit each pepper and remove the
core and seeds. Melt the butter in a
pan and cook the onion until soft.

2 To cook the couscous, bring
250 ml/8 fl oz/1 cup water to the
boil. Add the oil and the salt, then
remove the pan from the heat and
add the couscous. Stir and leave to
stand, covered, for 5 minutes. Stir in
the cooked onion, raisins and mint,
then season well with salt and pepper.
Stir in the egg yolk.

3 Using a teaspoon, fill the peppers
with the couscous mixture to only
about three-quarters full, as the
couscous will swell when cooked
further. Place in a lightly oiled
ovenproof dish and bake, uncovered,
for about 20 minutes until tender.
Serve hot or cold, garnished with the
mint leaves.

Aubergine Parmigiana

A classic Italian dish, in which sliced aubergines are layered with creamy Mozzarella, fresh Parmesan and a tomato sauce.

Serves 4–6

INGREDIENTS
3 medium aubergines, thinly sliced
olive oil, for brushing
300 g/11 oz Mozzarella cheese, sliced
115 g/4 oz/1⅓ cups freshly grated
   Parmesan cheese
30–45 ml/2–3 tbsp dried
   white breadcrumbs
salt and freshly ground black pepper
fresh basil sprigs, to garnish

FOR THE TOMATO SAUCE
30 ml/2 tbsp olive oil
1 onion, finely chopped
2 garlic cloves, crushed
400 g/14 oz can chopped tomatoes
5 ml/1 tsp granulated sugar
about 6 fresh basil leaves

1 Layer the aubergine slices in a colander, sprinkling each layer with a little salt. Leave for about 20 minutes, then rinse under cold running water and pat dry with kitchen paper.

2 Preheat the oven to 200°C/400°F/ Gas 6. Lay the aubergine slices on non-stick baking sheets, brush the tops with olive oil and bake for 10–15 minutes until softened.

3 To make the tomato sauce, heat the oil in a saucepan and sauté the onion and garlic for 5 minutes. Add the chopped tomatoes and sugar, with salt and pepper to taste. Bring to the boil, then lower the heat and simmer for about 10 minutes until reduced and thickened. Tear the basil leaves into small pieces and add them to the sauce.

4 Layer the aubergines in a greased, shallow, ovenproof dish with the sliced Mozzarella, tomato sauce and grated Parmesan, ending with a layer of Parmesan mixed with the dried breadcrumbs. Bake for 20–25 minutes until golden brown and bubbling. Allow to stand for 5 minutes before serving, garnished with basil sprigs.

Marinated Baby Aubergines with Raisins & Pine Nuts

Make this a day in advance, to allow the flavours to develop.

Serves 4

INGREDIENTS

12 baby aubergines,
   halved lengthways
250 ml/8 fl oz/1 cup extra-virgin
   olive oil
juice of 1 lemon
30 ml/2 tbsp balsamic vinegar
3 cloves
25 g/1 oz/¼ cup pine nuts
25 g/1 oz/2 tbsp raisins
15 ml/1 tbsp granulated sugar
1 bay leaf
large pinch of dried
   chilli flakes
salt and freshly ground
   black pepper

1 Preheat the grill to high. Place the aubergines, cut side up, in the grill pan and brush with a little of the olive oil. Grill for 10 minutes, until slightly blackened, turning them over halfway through cooking.

2 To make the marinade, put the remaining olive oil, the lemon juice, vinegar, cloves, pine nuts, raisins, sugar and bay leaf in a jug. Add the chilli flakes and salt and pepper and mix well.

3 Place the hot aubergines in an earthenware or glass bowl and pour over the marinade. Leave to cool, turning the aubergines once or twice. Serve cold.

Sautéed Courgettes Italian-style

The olive oil and fresh oregano give this dish a delicious fragrance.

Serves 4

INGREDIENTS
15 ml/1 tbsp olive oil
15 ml/1 tbsp sunflower oil
1 large onion, chopped
1 garlic clove, crushed
4–5 medium courgettes, cut into
    1 cm/½ in slices
150 ml/¼ pint/⅔ cup chicken or
    vegetable stock
2.5 ml/½ tsp chopped
    fresh oregano, plus extra, to garnish
salt and freshly ground black pepper

1 Heat the oils in a large frying pan and fry the onion and garlic over a moderate heat for 5–6 minutes until the onion has softened and is beginning to brown.

2 Add the courgettes and fry for about 4 minutes until they just start to be flecked with brown. Stir frequently.

3 Stir in the stock, oregano and seasoning and simmer gently for 8–10 minutes until the liquid has almost evaporated. Spoon the courgettes into a serving dish, sprinkle with oregano and serve.

Courgette Curry

Thickly sliced courgettes are combined with authentic Indian spices for a delicious, colourful vegetable curry.

Serves 4

INGREDIENTS
675 g/1½ lb courgettes
1 onion
45 ml/3 tbsp oil
2.5 ml/½ tsp cumin seeds
2.5 ml/½ tsp mustard seeds
2 garlic cloves, crushed
1.5 ml/¼ tsp ground turmeric
1.5 ml/¼ tsp chilli powder
5 ml/1 tsp ground coriander
5 ml/1 tsp ground cumin
2.5 ml/½ tsp salt
15 ml/1 tbsp tomato purée
400 g/14 oz can
    chopped tomatoes
150 ml/¼ pint/⅔ cup water
15 ml/1 tbsp chopped
    fresh coriander
5 ml/1 tsp garam masala

1 Trim the ends from the courgettes, then cut into 1 cm/½ in thick slices. Thinly slice the onion.

2 Heat the oil in a large saucepan and fry the cumin and mustard seeds for 2 minutes until they begin to splutter and pop.

3 Add the onion and garlic, and fry for about 5–6 minutes until the onion is beginning to soften.

4 Add the turmeric, chilli powder, ground coriander, cumin and salt, and fry for about 2–3 minutes.

5 Add the sliced courgettes all at once and cook for 5 minutes, stirring from time to time so that they are well coated with the spices.

6 Mix together the tomato purée and chopped tomatoes and add to the saucepan with the water. Cover and simmer for 10 minutes until the sauce thickens. Stir in the fresh coriander and garam masala, then cook for about 5 minutes or until the courgettes are tender. Serve immediately.

Baked Acorn Squash with Herbs

Each squash half holds a pool of fragrant melted herb butter.

Serves 4

INGREDIENTS
2 medium acorn squash
90 ml/6 tbsp chopped fresh mixed chives,
    thyme, basil and parsley
50 g/2 oz/4 tbsp butter
salt and freshly ground black pepper
fresh herbs, to garnish

1 Preheat the oven to 190°C/375°F/
Gas 5. Cut each squash in half
horizontally and scoop out the seeds
and stringy fibres. If necessary, cut a
small slice off the base of each half so
that it sits level.

2 Spoon a quarter of the herbs into
the hollow in each squash half. Top
each with 15 g/½ oz/1 tbsp butter and
season with salt and pepper.

3 Arrange the squash halves in a
shallow ovenproof dish large enough
to hold them in one layer. Pour
boiling water into the bottom of the
dish, to a depth of about 2.5 cm/1 in.
Cover loosely with a sheet of foil.

4 Bake for 45 minutes–1 hour until
the squash is tender when pierced.
Serve hot, keeping the halves upright,
garnished with fresh herbs.

Patty-pan Squash à la Grecque

Make the most of little patty-pan squashes with this traditional marinade.

Serves 4

INGREDIENTS
175 g/6 oz patty-pan squash
250 ml/8 fl oz/1 cup
   white wine
juice of 2 lemons
1 fresh thyme sprig
1 bay leaf
1 small bunch fresh chervil,
   roughly chopped
1.5 ml/¼ tsp coriander
   seeds, crushed
1.5 ml/¼ tsp black
   peppercorns, crushed
75 ml/5 tbsp olive oil
fresh herbs, to garnish

1 Blanch the patty-pan squash in boiling water for 3 minutes and then refresh them in cold water.

2 Place all the remaining ingredients in a pan, add 150 ml/½ pint/⅔ cup water and simmer for 10 minutes, covered. Add the patty-pans and cook for 10 minutes. Remove with a slotted spoon when they are cooked and tender to the bite.

3 Reduce the liquid by boiling hard for 10 minutes. Strain it and pour it over the squash. Leave until cool for the flavours to be absorbed. Serve cold, garnished with fresh herbs.

Pumpkin & Potato Pudding

Serve this savoury pudding with any rich meat dish or simply with a mixed salad.

Serves 4

INGREDIENTS
45 ml/3 tbsp olive oil
1 garlic clove, sliced
675 g/1½ lb pumpkin flesh, cut into
    2 cm/¾ in chunks
350 g/12 oz potatoes, unpeeled
25 g/1 oz/2 tbsp butter
90 g/3½ oz/scant ½ cup Ricotta cheese
50 g/2 oz/⅔ cup freshly grated
    Parmesan cheese
pinch of freshly grated nutmeg
4 medium eggs, separated
salt and freshly ground black pepper
chopped fresh herbs, to garnish

1 Preheat the oven to 200°C/400°F/ Gas 6. Grease a 1.75 litre/3 pint/ 7½ cup, shallow, oval baking dish.

2 Heat the oil in a large, shallow pan. Add the garlic and pumpkin chunks and cook, stirring often to prevent sticking, for 15–20 minutes or until the pumpkin is tender.

3 Meanwhile, cook the potatoes in boiling salted water for 20 minutes until tender. Drain, leave until cool enough to handle, then peel off the skins. Place the potatoes and pumpkin in a large bowl and mash well with the butter until smooth.

4 Mash the Ricotta with a fork until smooth, and add to the potato and pumpkin mixture, mixing well.

5 Stir in the Parmesan, nutmeg and plenty of salt and pepper. The mixture should be smooth and creamy. Add the egg yolks one at a time until mixed thoroughly.

VARIATION: When pumpkins are not available, this dish would work well using parsnips instead.

6 Whisk the egg whites with an electric whisk until they form stiff peaks, then fold gently into the mixture. Spoon into the prepared baking dish and bake for 30 minutes until golden and firm. Serve hot, garnished with herbs.

COOK'S TIP: Pumpkins can be stored for several months in a dry place. Once cut, store the unused part in the fridge and cover the cut side with clear film.

First published in 2000 by Hermes House

© Anness Publishing Limited 2000

Hermes House is an imprint of
Anness Publishing Limited
Hermes House
88-89 Blackfriars Road
London SE1 8HA

ISBN 1 84038 617 7

A CIP catalogue record for this book is available from the British Library

Publisher: Joanna Lorenz
Editor: Valerie Ferguson
Series Designer: Bobbie Colgate Stone
Designer: Andrew Heath
Editorial Reader: Hayley Kerr
Production Controller: Joanna King

Recipes Contributed by: Angela Boggiano, Carla Capalbo, Kit Chan, Carol Clements, Roz Denny, Patrizia Diemling,
Matthew Drennan, Joanna Farrow, Shirley Gill, Nicola Graimes, Rebekah Hassan, Christine Ingram, Manisha Kanina,
Lesley Mackley, Norma Miller, Sallie Morris, Annie Nichols, Katherine Richmond, Liz Trigg, Laura Washburn,
Elizabeth Wolf-Cohen, Jenni Wright.

Photography: James Duncan, John Freeman, Michelle Garrett, John Heseltine, Amanda Heywood, Janine Hosegood,
David Jordan, William Lingwood, Patrick McLeavey, Michael Michaels, Thomas Odulate.

1 3 5 7 9 10 8 6 4 2

Notes:
For all recipes, quantities are given in both metric and imperial measures and,
where appropriate, measures are also given in standard cups and spoons.
Follow one set, but not a mixture, because they are
not interchangeable.
Standard spoon and cup measures are level.
1 tsp = 5 ml   1 tbsp = 15 ml
1 cup = 250 ml/8 fl oz
Australian standard tablespoons are 20 ml.
Australian readers should use 3 tsp in place of 1 tbsp for measuring small quantities of gelatine,
cornflour, salt, etc.
Medium eggs are used unless otherwise stated.

Printed and bound in China